D1040451

Romsdal Snow.

Rain does not remain
in the clouds for long.

Norwegian Proverbs

Collected by Joanne Asala
from the Stories of
Peter Christian Asbjørnsen
and Jørgen Moe

Engravings of Norway from the book
"Gamle Norge" or
Rambles and Scrambles in Norway
by Robert Taylor Pritchett
Virtue & Co. Limited, 1879
Engravings by Messrs. J. & G. Nicholls,

Penfield
Books

About the Editor

Joanne Asala is a writer and editor dedicated to the preservation of traditional customs. Of Finnish and Polish descent, she grew up in Bloomingdale, Illinois, a suburb of Chicago, and earned a degree in English from the University of Iowa with an emphasis in Medieval Studies. Her titles for Penfield Press include *Swedish Proverbs, Words of Wisdom from the Vikings,* and *Trolls Remembering Norway.*

Acknowledgments

A special thank you goes to Darrell Henning, Director of Vesterheim, The Norwegian-American Museum, Decorah, Iowa, and to Carol Hasvold, Librarian/Registrar.

Cover photographs from the Vesterheim collection, which include objects from the former Luther College collection, are by Joan Liffring-Zug. On the front is an Ølkjeng (two-handled ale bowl) carved and painted by Jon Endreson Folkedal in Granvin, Norway, in 1816. His stepson Svein brought the bowl to Winneshiek County, Iowa, in 1857. It was last used for drinking toasts at a Folkedal family wedding in the 1970s. Donated by John Haltmeyer of Stoddard, Wisconsin in memory of his wife, Adeline Johnson Haltmeyer. The bowl sits on a Fremskap (sideboard) made of pine. Painted by Peder Veggum of the Gudbrandsdal area in the 18th century. Gift of Maihaugen Museum in Norway.

The back cover shows an Ambar (porridge container) made of birch in 1820. Donated by Tynset Museum, Norway. Early 19th-century birch Ølbolle (large ale bowl), Telemark. Ølkanne (ale tankard) made of pine staves. Signed, Sander Sandersen Raaen, 1853. Donated by a Norwegian immigrant family. Small plates, turned of birch, 19th-century Norwegian. Teppe (coverlet), woven of wool and linen in the 19th century. From a farm near Trondheim. Donated by Mrs. Roger Tallaksen, Minneapolis, Minnesota.

Edited by John Zug and Dorothy Crum. Graphic design by Robyn Loughran.

Books by Mail: $14.95 each, postpaid. Prices subject to change.
Norwegian Proverbs (this book)   *Scandinavian Proverbs*
For a catalog of titles available, please send $2.00 to:
Penfield Books, 215 Brown Street, Iowa City, IA 52245

Table of Contents

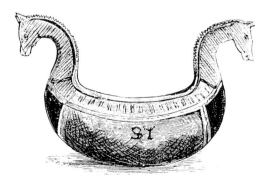

Wooden Bridge at Roldal.

Who are Asbjørnsen and Moe?

Norwegian folktales were first written down in the 1830s. Inspired by the Germanic fairy tales of the Brothers Grimm, two students—Peter Christian Asbjørnsen and Jørgen Moe—prepared a similar volume of the folktales and legends of their native land. In a letter to Jacob Grimm they wrote, "An early acquaintanceship with your *Kinder und Hausmärchen*, as well as an intimate knowledge of the life and lore of the people of Norway, gave us the idea to prepare a collection of Norwegian folktales."

However, Asbjørnsen and Moe departed from the ornate literary style of the Grimms' tales. They decided that the stories should be written in a popular style, one which would stay as close as possible to the language, humor, vitality and colloquialisms of the tales as they were told in the mountains and vast forests of Norway.

For the first time, Norwegian common speech appeared in print, and the stories reflected the strong imagination, independence and self-reliance of the peasant class. Included in these tales were the native bits of wisdom—the proverbs—of everyday life.

The first volume of their tales, *Norske Folkeeventyr,* appeared in 1845, with a second edition in 1852. The tales became enormously popular and were translated into many languages. As a result, Asbjørnsen and Moe continued their research, and traveled throughout the various districts of Norway gathering and retelling the folktales, although they had to make time for other careers to earn a living; Asbjørnsen became a zoologist and a forest inspector and Moe a clergyman and bishop.

The two friends published additional volumes of their work, and many of the stories appeared in newspapers and magazines.

When Moe's clerical duties took him away from his work in the field, his son, Moltke, continued the work of his father.

The publication of *Norske Folkeeventyr* had a huge impact on the Norwegian people. As the *Kalevala* helped shape the independent spirit of the Finnish people, so too did the tales of Asbjørnsen and Moe help the Norwegians realize that even during the days of Danish dominance, the people were able to keep hold of their own legends and beliefs, and to present the world with a set of stories that were all their own.

Sea Warehouse: Molde.

The Norwegians and Spectacular Scenery

Sanøe, looking down the valley.

Every man is free
to believe what he wants.

Hellesylt.

Interior of Molmen Church.

It is a narrow way
which leadeth unto the
kingdom of heaven.

Skjæggedal Fos.

The Troltinderne by Moonlight.

The Lord is high above us
and the king is far away.

When a big stone rolls
    it carries many
        along with it.

Snow Pass: Thorbvu.

*You don't know what a man
is made of until
he encounters hardship.*

After sport.

He who cannot climb up
cannot climb down.

A man is often more
than he wishes.

The morning hour
has a golden dower.

Volda.

He who follows the river
comes at last to the sea.

Courtship
and Marriage

Hitterdal Church.

Rauma River Boat.

A lover should open his ears
more than his eyes.

A woman's counsel
is always worth having.

Silence is sometimes
an answer.

The Spring Dance: Hardanger.

Everything that men undertake
requires a helping hand.

TRue love does not grow rusty.

Before the Wedding.

A Bridal Party crossing the Fjord.

The Bride's Return by Water.

Having a woman
who loves you is better
than owning gold or goods.

The word that lies nearest
the heart
comes first to life.

Blessed are the Children

Return from the Christening.

Never quarrel about
a baby's name
before it is born.

The Lych Gate, Nordfjord.
A new mother is given rømmegrøt.

One's own children
are always prettiest.

The Friendly Toilette.

All good things
        come in threes.

No one knows how children
will turn out;
        a great tree often springs
            from a slender plant.

A child learns to speak
        quicker than he
            learns to keep silent.

Do not despise the children
    of the poor and needy,
for none can tell
        how they may turn out.

It is safer in your mother's lap
    than in a nobleman's bed.

What mother and father
    don't teach, the world teaches.

Hitterdal Church: Sunday Morning.

Eieksdal.

Comforts of Home

Haugen, near Hellesylt.

A home is a home
be it ever so homely.

Worm box.

A Good Beginning.

Every man's home is his castle.

TRY all the world 'round,
there's nothing like home.

Carved House in Thelemarken.

'Tis good to travel east
and west, but after all
a home is best.

Maritz Sæter.

The Laave at Fiva: Romsdal.

Flatdal: Thelemarken.

IT IS BETTER TO SIT
        on one's own perch,
FOR THEN one can never be
                LEFT IN THE LURCH.

Seljestad.

All cocks crow loudest at home.

That house will never
have a clock
where there is neither
dog nor cock.

Unexpected guests are
not always welcome.

It isn't easy to sit
on a borrowed chair.

Carved Houses, Bru, Thelemarken.

Friends and Neighbors

The Market: Bergen.

Sledging.

With gossip and gabble is built
neither house nor stable.

Good neighbors make
good friends.

Luck and Misfortune
are neighbors.

As one selects his company,
so one is rewarded.

The Stolkjær and Boat.

Tongues will clack
      behind one's back.

Self-help is
      the best help.

Flapping and crowing
      sets tongues a-going.

Faleidet: Nordfjord.

It is better to live
    in a good neighborhood
        than to be widely known.

A good neighbor is better than
    a sister in the next village.

Bergen: Fish Market in the distance.

The World of Work

The Flower Market: Molde.

With fair words and money, one can go far in a day.

Wool Holder.

Work done in haste
    will never last.

One who lives long
            always finds
    enough work to do.

Spinning in the sæter: Isterdal.

Syltebø: with Farm Implements.

What a man sows he shall reap.

Good tools make good work.

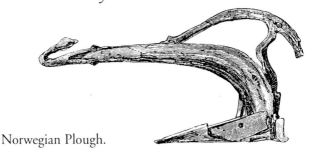

Norwegian Plough.

The Meal Mill: Isterdal.

The Saw-Mill: Udvig.

Money
brings money.

The Post arriving at Udvig.

The best servant is one's own self.

The Raft Boat: Thelemarken.

Postman and his Carriole.

The Coast Inspector.

He who will ever
taste and try
will burn his fingers
in the pie.

Shipping a Carriole.

Necessity
teaches new arts.

Carriole crossing a River.

Bergen.

I⊤'s chilð's play
when ⊤HRee
share ⊤He ðay.

Good company
is a comfort.

The Courtyard, Victoria Hotel, Christiania.

Worldly Advice

The Eagle's Nest.

He that swaps
with a bear
always comes
worst off.

An old fox
is hard to hunt.

He who lays traps
for others
comes into the trap
himself.

Making for the Fjord.

Many become brave
        when cornered.

One learns
        as long as one lives.

By cunning and skill
even a lame man
can do what he will.

No one hides
honest money.

The man who has
as much money as he wishes
is always sure
to get on in the world.

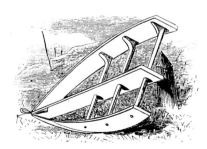

Snow Plough.

The Landing-place: Molde.

He is worth much who has learned much.

Old habits have deep roots.

Envy does more harm
       to its owner
             than to anyone else.

S leep is
       the biggest thief,
it thinks nothing
             of stealing
                   half one's life.

He who samples everything
       will taste
             both sweet and sour.

A little share now
        is better than
                a long lawsuit.

They are not
        all thieves
    at whom the dog barks.

All are not beggars
        who are
                tattered and torn.

What is honest never sinks.

If there were no fools, how would we recognize the wise?

Christiansand.

Reindeer Antlers.

One can't go far without meat, for meat is man's strength.

Near Ovendal: after Reindeer.

When All is Done

The Churchyard: Molde.

Everyone is nearest
to his own self.

Gray hair should be
respected and honored,
a bald head deserves
a bow.

While there's life,
there's hope.

Tears never yet
dug up anyone from his grave.

Hard things are said
of a man
when he's dead.

The Funeral: Bergen.

There's a cure and
    physic for everything
            but death.

Death has no cure.

What's done is done.

List of Consulted Sources

Asbjørnsen, Peter Christian; Moe, Jørgen. Translated by Pat Shaw and Carl Norman. *Norwegian Folk Tales*. New York, 1960.

Asbjørnsen, Peter Christian. Translated by G.W. Dasent. *Tales from the Fjeld*. London, 1874.

Asbjørnsen, Peter Christian; Moe, Jørgen. Translated by G.W. Dasent. *Popular Tales from the Norse*. Edinburgh, 1888.

Asbjørnsen, Peter Christian; Moe, Jørgen. Translated by Joan Roll-Hansen. *A Time for Trolls*. Oslo, 1962.

Stabur and Wooden Tankards.